TREATs

just great recipes

GENERAL INFORMATION
The level of difficulty of the recipes in this book
is expressed as a number from 1 (simple) to 3 (difficult).

TREATS
just great recipes

finger food

McRae Books

Eggplant Dip
with toast

Preheat the oven to 400°F (200°C/gas 6). • Prick the eggplants all over with a fork and place them on a baking sheet. • Bake for 1 hour, or until softened. • Scoop out the flesh with a spoon and mash with a fork in a medium bowl. • Mix in the garlic, tahini, lemon juice, and salt. • Garnish with the parsley. • Serve warm with triangles of toasted bread or tortilla chips.

2 large eggplants (aubergines)

2 cloves garlic, finely chopped

2 tablespoons sesame seed paste (tahini)

Juice of 1 lemon

Salt

2 tablespoons finely chopped parsley

Onion Dip
with fresh vegetables

Place the sour cream and cheese in a medium bowl. • Add the soup mix and stir until smooth. Season with the pepper. • Cover the bowl and chill in the refrigerator for at least 2 hours. • Serve with a selection of chopped raw vegetables (or with potato chips, crackers, or squares of freshly toasted bread).

2 cups (500 ml) sour cream
3 oz (90 g) Cheddar cheese, finely grated
1 package dry onion soup mix
Freshly ground white pepper

SERVES 8–10

PREPARATION 10 min + 2 h to rest

DIFFICULTY level 1

Green Olives

with spicy dressing

Rinse the olives in cold water and pat dry with paper towels. • Lightly crush the olives with a meat-pounding mallet. • Use the same instrument to bruise the cloves of garlic. Place the olives and garlic in a serving bowl. • Remove the rosemary leaves from the sprig and chop coarsely. Add to the olives, together with the oregano, chile peppers, and oil. Mix well and cover. Set aside in a cool place (not the refrigerator) for at least 2 hours before serving. • Serve with freshly baked bread.

12 oz (350 g) green olives, preserved in brine, pitted
4 cloves garlic, peeled
1 sprig fresh rosemary
1 teaspoon teaspoon oregano
1–2 dried red chile peppers, crumbled
1/4 cup (60 g) extra-virgin olive oil

SERVES 6–8

PREPARATION 20 min + 1 h to rest

COOKING 20 min

DIFFICULTY level 2

Brussels Sprouts
filled with herb cream

Cook the sprouts and vinegar in a large pan of lightly salted, boiling water until just tender, 5–7 minutes. Drain well. • Coarsely chop one-third of the Brussels sprouts. Use a teaspoon to hollow the centers out of the remaining sprouts. • Heat 2 tablespoons of butter in a large frying pan and sauté the garlic until pale gold, 2–3 minutes. Add the chopped sprouts, herbs, and cream. Season with salt and pepper and simmer over low heat, stirring frequently, for 10 minutes. • Place the hollow sprouts in another pan with the remaining butter. Season with salt and pepper and simmer over low heat for 10 minutes. • Use a teaspoon to fill the sprouts. Top each sprout with a small piece of bell pepper. • Serve hot or at room temperature.

1 lb (500 g) fresh or frozen Brussels sprouts

1 tablespoon white wine vinegar

1/4 cup (60 g) butter

1 clove garlic, finely chopped

4 tablespoons finely chopped mixed fresh herbs (parsley, dill, basil, tarragon, marjoram, etc)

1/4 cup (60 ml) heavy (double) cream

Salt and freshly ground black pepper

1 small red bell pepper (capsicum), cleaned and cut in tiny squares, to garnish

SERVES 4

PREPARATION 15 min

COOKING 15 min

DIFFICULTY level 1

Fresh Celery
with blue cheese and ricotta

Place the ricotta in a bowl. Add the blue cheese and milk and mash to obtain a fairly smooth cream. • Add the garlic, chives, oil, salt, and pepper. Mix well. • Cover and chill in the refrigerator for 1 hour. • Trim the celery stalks and remove any tough external fibers. Cut into pieces about 3 inches (8 cm) long. • Fill the celery with the cheese mixture, sprinkle with the parsley and serve.

8 oz (250 g) fresh ricotta cheese, drained
4 oz (125 g) blue cheese, crumbled into small pieces
1/4 cup (60 g) milk
2 cloves garlic, finely chopped
1 tablespoon finely chopped chives
1 tablespoon extra-virgin olive oil
Salt and freshly ground black pepper
10 large stalks very fresh celery
1 tablespoon finely chopped parsley

SERVES 6–8

PREPARATION 20 min

DIFFICULTY level 1

Cherry Tomatoes
with tuna, mayo, and walnuts

Slice the tops off the tomatoes. Use a teaspoon to scoop out the flesh and seeds. Sprinkle the insides with salt. Drain the tomatoes cut-side down on paper towels for 15 minutes. • Place the tuna, mayonnaise, capers, anchovies, garlic, oregano, basil, walnuts, and the ice cube in the bowl of a food processor. Chop until smooth. • Season with salt and stir in the Parmesan. Mix well. Fill the tomatoes with this mixture. • Arrange on a serving plate and serve.

24 cherry tomatoes
Salt
5 oz (150 g) canned tuna, drained
$1/4$ cup (60 g) mayonnaise
1 tablespoon salt-cured capers, rinsed
2 anchovy fillets, rinsed
2 cloves garlic, peeled
2 sprigs fresh oregano
Handful fresh basil leaves
$1/3$ cup (50 g) shelled walnuts
1 ice cube
$1/2$ cup (60 g) freshly grated Parmesan

SERVES 8

PREPARATION 15 min + 30 min to chill

COOKING 10 min

DIFFICULTY level 1

Mushroom Toasts

Sauté the mushrooms and garlic in 2 tablespoons of oil in a frying pan over medium heat until the mushrooms are tender and the cooking juices they release have evaporated, 7–10 minutes. Remove from the heat and let cool. • Place the mushrooms in a food processor or blender with the cheese and enough of the remaining oil to make a smooth cream. • Season with salt and chill in the refrigerator for 30 minutes. • Spread the cream over the toasted bread and serve.

12 oz (350 g) white mushrooms, finely chopped
2 cloves garlic, finely chopped
4–6 tablespoons extra-virgin olive oil
3/4 cup (180 g) fresh creamy cheese (mascarpone, cream cheese)
Salt
8 slices toasted bread

SERVES 8–10

PREPARATION 15 min + 15 min to drain

DIFFICULTY level 1

Cherry Tomatoes
with tzatziki

Slice the tops off the tomatoes. Use a teaspoons to scoop out the flesh and seeds. Sprinkle the insides with salt. Drain the tomatoes cut-side down on paper towels for 15 minutes. • Peel and grate the cucumbers. Sprinkle with salt and drain in a colander. Squeeze out the extra moisture. • Mix the yogurt, garlic, cucumber, and mint in a medium bowl. Add the oil and stir until well mixed. Season with salt. • Spoon the mixture into the tomatoes. Arrange the filled tomatoes on a serving dish and serve at once.

20–24 cherry tomatoes
Salt
2 small cucumbers
$3/4$ cup (180 g) Greek (thick, creamy) plain yogurt
3 cloves garlic, finely chopped
1 tablespoon finely chopped fresh mint
2 tablespoons extra-virgin olive oil

SERVES 8–10

PREPARATION 25 min

COOKING 20 min

DIFFICULTY level 1

Vol-Au-Vents

with cream sauce and shrimps

Preheat the oven to 400°F (200°C/gas 6). • Oil a large baking dish and line with waxed paper. • Bring a medium pan of salted water to a boil over medium-high heat. • Plunge in the shrimp tails and cook for 1 minute. Drain and let cool. Peel and coarsely chop half the shrimp tails. • Melt the butter in a small pan over low heat. Add the flour and cook over low heat for 2 minutes, stirring constantly. • Remove from the heat and pour in the milk all at once. Stir constantly over low heat until thickened, 5–7 minutes. • Remove from the heat and stir in the chopped shrimp, lemon juice, chives, paprika, salt, and pepper. • Fill the cases with the shrimp mixture. Decorate some of the vol-au-vents with the whole shrimp tails. Arrange in the prepared dish. • Bake until the pastry is golden brown, 10 minutes. • Serve hot or at room temperature.

36 small shrimp (prawn) tails, deveined
2 tablespoons butter
3 tablespoons all-purpose (plain) flour
1 cup (250 ml) milk
Few drops freshly squeezed lemon juice
1 tablespoon finely chopped chives
1 teaspoon sweet paprika
Salt and freshly ground black pepper
24 small vol-au-vent cases

Rice Tartlets
with zucchini

Preheat the oven to 350°F (180°C/gas 4). • Oil two 6-cup muffin pans. • Dough: Sift the flour and salt into a bowl. Mix in the milk, water, and oil. Shape into a ball. • Filling: Bring the milk and salt to a boil in a medium saucepan. • Add the rice and simmer until tender, 15–20 minutes. • Sauté the shallot in the oil in a frying pan until softened, 4–5 minutes. • Add the zucchini and cook for 5 minutes. Season with salt. • If using zucchini flowers, blanch in a large pot of boiling water for 5 seconds. Drain well. • Stir the zucchini mixture into the rice. • Add the eggs, Parmesan, oregano, and nutmeg. Season with pepper. • Roll the dough out thinly. Cut out rounds to line the pans. Fill with the rice mixture and top with a zucchini flower, if using. Dot with the butter. • Bake until set and golden brown, 15–20 minutes. • Serve warm.

Pastry
1²/₃ cups (250 g) all-purpose (plain) flour
¹/₈ teaspoon salt
¹/₃ cup (90 ml) milk
3 tablespoons water
3 tablespoons extra-virgin olive oil

Filling
4 cups (1 liter) milk
¹/₄ teaspoon salt
³/₄ cup (150 g) rice
2 shallots, finely chopped
2 tablespoons extra-virgin olive oil
4 zucchini (courgettes), finely chopped
Salt and freshly ground black pepper
12 small zucchini flowers (optional)
2 eggs, lightly beaten
³/₄ cup (100 g) freshly grated Parmesan
¹/₂ teaspoon dried oregano
¹/₄ teaspoon freshly ground nutmeg
2 tablespoons butter, cut up

Vol-Au-Vents
with vegetables and olives

Preheat the oven to 350°F (180°C/gas 4). • Oil a large baking sheet.
• Heat the oil in a large frying pan over medium heat. Add the shallot
and sauté until transparent, 2–3 minutes. • Add the carrots, zucchini,
and peas. Sauté for 5 minutes. • Add the wine and sauté until
evaporated, 3–4 minutes. • Add the thyme and season with salt.
Cook until the vegetables are tender, 7–8 minutes. • Stir in the olives
and simmer until heated through, 2 minutes. • Arrange the vol-au-
vents on the baking sheet. • Bake until golden brown, 10–15 minutes.
• Spoon the filling into the vol-au-vent cases. • Serve hot.

$1/4$ cup (60 ml) extra-virgin olive oil
1 shallot, finely chopped
3 carrots, finely chopped
3 zucchini (courgettes), finely chopped
1 cup (150 g) frozen peas
$1/3$ cup (90 ml) dry white wine
$1/2$ teaspoon dried thyme
Salt
12 green olives, pitted and chopped
12 frozen vol-au-vent cases

SERVES 6–8

PREPARATION 15 min

COOKING 20 min

DIFFICULTY level 1

Vol-Au-Vents
with leek, egg, and pesto

Preheat the oven to 400°F(200°C/gas 6). • Arrange the pastry cases on a baking sheet. • Bake until risen and golden brown, about 10 minutes. • Let cool slightly. • Meanwhile, sauté the leek in the butter in a large frying pan over medium heat until softened, about 5 minutes. • Beat the eggs and milk in a large bowl. Season with salt and pepper. • Pour the mixture into the frying pan. Simmer for 2–3 minutes, stirring constantly, until the egg is cooked. • Spoon the mixture into the pastry cases. Top each one with a little pesto and garnish with the pine nuts and basil. • Serve at once.

16 small vol-au-vent cases, frozen
White part of 1 leek, finely sliced
2 tablespoons butter
4 large eggs, lightly beaten
2 tablespoons milk
Salt and freshly ground black pepper
$1/2$ cup (125 ml) readymade pesto
    (Italian basil sauce)
2 tablespoons pine nuts
Basil leaves, to garnish

Spinach Tart
with feta cheese and dill

Preheat the oven to 400°F (200°C/gas 6). • Oil a 9-inch (23-cm) square baking pan. • Heat the oil in a large frying pan over medium heat. Sauté the scallions in the oil until softened, about 5 minutes. • Add the spinach, season with salt and pepper, and simmer over low heat until tender, 7–10 minutes. • Remove from the heat and stir in the feta, dill, and eggs. • Place a sheet of phyllo in the baking pan and brush with butter, Cover with two sheets of phyllo, brushing each one with butter. • Spoon the spinach filling over the top. Cover with a sheet of phyllo and brush with butter. Repeat with the remaining sheets of phyllo, tucking the edges down into the filling to seal the pie. • Use a sharp knife to cut into squares. • Bake until risen and golden brown, 30–35 minutes. • Serve hot.

3 tablespoons extra-virgin olive oil

3 scallions (spring onions),
finely chopped

2 lb (1 kg) frozen spinach

Salt and freshly ground black pepper

8 oz (250 g) feta cheese,
cut into small cubes

4 tablespoons finely chopped fresh dill

2 large eggs, lightly beaten

6 sheets phyllo pasta

1/2 cup (125 g) butter, melted

SERVES 8–10

PREPARATION 30 min

COOKING 50 min

DIFFICULTY level 2

Ricotta Tart
with vegetables and herbs

Preheat the oven to 400°F (200°C/gas 6). • Oil a 10-inch (25-cm) round baking pan. • Heat the oil in a large frying pan over medium heat. Sauté the leeks in the oil until softened, about 5 minutes. • Add the carrots and sauté for 5 minutes. • Place the ricotta in a large bowl and stir in the 2 eggs, mixed herbs, cheese, and vegetable mixture. Season with salt and pepper and mix well. • Roll out two-thirds of the pastry and press into the bottom and sides of the prepared pan. • Spoon the filling into the pan. • Roll out the remaining pastry and cut into long thin strips. Arrange over the pan in a lattice patter. • Mix the remaining egg with the milk and brush the top of the tart. • Bake until set and golden brown, 35–40 minutes. • Serve warm.

14 oz (400 g) frozen shortcrust pastry, thawed

2 tablespoons extra-virgin olive oil

2 leeks, thinly sliced

2 carrots, cut in small cubes

1 lb (500 g) ricotta cheese, drained

3 tablespoons finely chopped mixed herbs (parsley, sage, thyme)

2 large eggs, lightly beaten + 1 extra, to brush

1/2 cup (60 g) freshly grated Parmesan

Salt and freshly ground black pepper

2 tablespoons milk

Smoked Salmon
rolls with goat cheese

Cut the rolls in half and remove some of the soft part from inside.
• Use a fork to beat together the goat cheese and cream cheese in
a medium bowl. • Mix in the parsley, chives, and oil. Season with salt
and pepper. • Fill the rolls with the cheese mixture and cover with
a slice of smoked salmon. • Serve at once.

12 mini bread rolls
¾ cup (180 g) soft fresh goat cheese
4 tablespoons cream cheese
1 tablespoon finely chopped parsley
2 teaspoon snipped chives
2 tablespoons extra-virgin olive oil
Salt and freshly ground black pepper
8 oz (250 g) smoked salmon

SERVES 6

PREPARATION 15 min + 4 h to marinate

DIFFICULTY level 1

Crostini
with bell peppers

Broil (grill) or roast the bell peppers whole until the skins are blackened. • Wrap them in a paper bag for 5 minutes, then remove the skins and seeds. Rinse carefully and dry on a clean cloth. • Slice the bell peppers into small, thin strips and place in a large bowl. Add the garlic, basil, olives, oil, salt, and pepper and marinate in the refrigerator for 4 hours. • Spread the bell pepper mixture on the freshly toasted bread and serve.

1 red bell pepper (capsicum)
1 yellow bell pepper (capsicum)
1 clove garlic, finely chopped
4 leaves basil, torn
2 tablespoons pitted black olives, coarsely chopped
1/4 cup (60 ml) extra-virgin olive oil
Salt and freshly ground black pepper
1 baguette (French loaf), sliced and toasted

Crostini
with goat cheese

Mix the goat cheese, scallion, and oil in a small bowl to make a smooth paste. Season with salt and pepper. Mix well. • Spread the toast with the butter. • Spread each piece of toast with the cheese mixture. Arrange the crostini on a serving plate. • Serve while the toast is still warm.

1 cup (250 g) fresh creamy goat cheese

2 scallions (green onions), finely sliced

2 tablespoons extra-virgin olive oil

Salt and freshly ground black pepper

1 baguette (French loaf), sliced and toasted

2 tablespoons butter

Mixed Crostini

Preheat the broiler (grill) to a medium setting. • Beat together the Parmesan and 3 tablespoons of butter in a small bowl. • Mix the Gorgonzola with 6 tablespoons of honey in another small bowl with a fork to make a smooth paste. • Mix the chopped walnuts with 3 tablespoons of honey and the mustard in another small bowl. • Process the olives with 1 tablespoon of honey and the lemon juice until smooth. • Toast the bread under the broiler until golden. • Spread 16 slices with the remaining honey. Spread 8 slices with the Parmesan mixture. Garnish with a slice of pear and a walnut. Spread the other 8 with the remaining butter. Top with the prosciutto. • Spread another 8 slices with the olive mixture and garnish with the lemon zest. • Spread another 8 slices with the Gorgonzola mixture and garnish with the celery. • Spread the remaining 8 toasts with the mustard mixture. Arrange the crostini a large serving and serve.

3/4 cup (100 g) freshly grated Parmesan
1/4 cup (60 g) butter
5 oz (150 g) Gorgonzola cheese, diced
3/4 cup (180 ml) clear honey
3/4 cup (75 g) chopped walnuts
2 tablespoons wholegrain mustard
3/4 cup (75 g) black olives, pitted
Juice of 1 lemon
40 small slices crusty bread
1 large ripe pear, peeled, cored, and sliced
8 walnuts
8 slices prosciutto (Parma ham)
Zest of 1 lemon, finely sliced
1 stalk celery, thinly sliced

Cheese Toasts

with pears and hazelnuts

Preheat the broiler (grill) to a high setting. • Melt the butter in a frying pan over medium heat. Add the shallot and sauté until translucent, 3–4 minutes. Set aside. • Add the pear to the frying pan and sauté for 2 minutes. • Add the wine and let it evaporate for 1 minute. Remove from the heat and drain the pears on paper towels. Sprinkle with the cinnamon and let cool slightly. • Toast the bread under the broiler until golden brown. • Lay the brie on the toasted bread. Add a layer of shallots and a layer of pear. • Broil until the cheese is melted, 2–3 minutes. Season with salt and pepper. • Sprinkle with the parsley and hazelnuts. Serve hot.

3 tablespoons butter
1 shallot, finely chopped
2 large slightly underripe pears, peeled, cored, and sliced
1/4 cup (60 ml) sweet white wine
1/2 teaspoon ground cinnamon
8–10 slices sandwich bread
8 oz (250 g) brie, sliced
Salt and freshly ground black pepper
1 tablespoon finely chopped parsley
2/3 cup (75 g) chopped hazelnuts

Pastry Hearts
with pine nuts and parmesan

Preheat the oven to 350°F (180°C/gas 4). • Oil a large baking sheet. • Roll out the pastry on a lightly floured work surface to ¼ inch (5 mm) thick. • Brush with the egg yolk. Sprinkle with the pine nuts and Parmesan. • Roll up the pastry starting from one edge and rolling until you reach the center. Roll up the remaining pastry starting from the opposite edge to make a double roll. • Chill the pastry roll in the refrigerator for 45 minutes. • Use a sharp knife to cut into slices ¼ inch (5 mm) thick. Arrange on the baking sheet. • Bake until golden brown, 10–15 minutes. • Serve hot or at room temperature.

6 oz (180 g) frozen puff pastry, thawed
1 large egg yolk, beaten
¼ cup (45 g) pine nuts
½ cup (60 g) freshly grated Parmesan

SERVES 6–8

PREPARATION 15 min

COOKING 15 min

DIFFICULTY level 1

Little Pizzas

with tomato and anchovies

Preheat the oven to 350°F (180°C/gas 4). • Oil a large baking sheet. • Roll out the pastry on a lightly floured work surface to 1/4 inch (5 mm) thick. • Cut the pastry into 2 1/2-inch (6-cm) disks, using a cookie cutter or a glass. Arrange the disks on the baking sheet. • Top each disk with a slice of tomato, half an anchovy fillet, and a pinch of oregano. Season with salt and pepper. • Bake until the pastry is golden brown, 10–15 minutes. • Serve hot.

6 oz (180 g) frozen puff pastry, thawed
2–3 large ripe tomatoes, thinly sliced
20 anchovy fillets preserved in oil, drained and halved
1/2 teaspoon dried oregano
salt and freshly ground black pepper

SERVES 6–8

PREPARATION 15 min + 2 h for dough

COOKING 15 min

DIFFICULTY level 1

Focaccia

with cherry tomatoes and basil

Pizza Dough: Place the fresh or active dry yeast in a small bowl and add half the warm water. Stir gently until the yeast has dissolved. Set aside for 15 minutes. • Place the flour and salt in a large bowl. Pour in the yeast mixture and the most of the remaining water and stir well. • Place the dough on a lightly floured work surface and knead gently and with the lightest possible touch until the dough is smooth and elastic, about 10 minutes. • Shape into a ball and place in a large oiled bowl. Set aside to rise until doubled in volume, about 90 minutes. • Preheat the oven to 400°F (200°C/gas 6). • Oil a rectangular baking pan about 10 x 15 inches (25 x 38 cm) in size. • When the rising time has elapsed, use your fingertips to press the dough into the baking pan. • Place the tomatoes on top, cut side up, pressing them into the dough. Drizzle with half the oil. Season with salt and pepper. • Bake until golden brown, 15–20 minutes. • Drizzle with the remaining oil and garnish with the basil. • Cut into small pieces. • Serve hot or at room temperature.

Pizza Dough
1 oz (30 g) fresh yeast or 2 ($^1/_4$-oz/7-g) packages active dry yeast
About $^2/_3$ cup (150 ml) warm water
3 cups (450 g) all-purpose (plain) flour
$^1/_2$ teaspoon salt

Topping
12 oz (350 g) cherry tomatoes, cut in half and seeded
2–4 tablespoons extra-virgin olive oil
Salt and freshly ground black pepper
Fresh mint, to garnish

Little Pizzas
with ricotta and zucchini

Prepare the pizza dough. • Heat the oil in a large frying pan over medium heat. Sauté the zucchini, zucchini flowers, and scallion until softened, about 5 minutes. Season with salt and pepper. • Beat the ricotta, eggs, and thyme in a large bowl. • Preheat the oven to 400°F (200°C/gas 6). • Roll the dough out thinly on a lightly floured work surface. Divide into ten equal parts and line ten 4-inch (10-cm) tartlet pans. Let rise for 15 minutes. • Mix the zucchini and pistachios into the ricotta mixture. Reserve a little of the zucchini mixture to garnish. Spoon the mixture evenly into the pans. • Bake for 10 minutes. • Lower the temperature to 350°F (180°C/gas 4) and bake for 10 minutes more, or until golden. • Garnish with the reserved zucchini mixture and serve hot.

1 quantity pizza dough (see page 32)
1 lb (500 g) zucchini (courgettes), preferably with flowers, thinly sliced
1 scallion (green onion), finely sliced
2 tablespoons extra-virgin olive oil
Salt and freshly ground black pepper
1¼ cups (310 g) ricotta cheese
2 eggs
1 tablespoon finely chopped thyme
½ cup (50 g) chopped pistachios

SERVES 4–6

PREPARATION 20 min + 2 h for dough

COOKING 20 min

DIFFICULTY level 2

Filled Pizzas
with tomatoes and parmesan

Prepare the pizza dough. • When the rising time has elapsed, divide into 12 pieces and shape into balls. Cover with a cloth and let rise for 15 minutes. • Roll the dough balls out on a lightly floured work surface into ¼-inch (5-mm) thick disks. • Heat the oil in a large frying pan to very hot. • Fry the pizzas in small batches until golden, spooning the oil over them. This will help them swell up. • Drain well on paper towels. • Cut a slice into the sides of the pizzas and spoon in the tomato sauce. Sprinkle with the Parmesan, basil, and oregano and serve hot.

1 quantity pizza dough (see page 32)
2 cups (500 ml) olive oil, for frying
1 (14-oz/400-g) can storebought tomato sauce (for pasta or pizza))
1 cup (125 g) freshly grated Parmesan
2 tablespoons finely chopped basil
1 teaspoon dried oregano

SERVES 6–8

PREPARATION 20 min + 2 h for dough

COOKING 25–30 min

DIFFICULTY level 1

Pizza Triangles

with onion, cheese, and olives

Prepare the pizza dough. • Peel the onions and slice thinly. • Cook the onions with the water, 2 tablespoons of oil, and the thyme and rosemary in a large frying pan over medium heat until all the liquid has evaporated, 5–10 minutes. • Season with salt, remove from the heat, and let cool. • Preheat the oven to 4505°F (220°C/gas 8). • Oil a large baking sheet. • When the rising time has elapsed, roll the dough out about 1/8 inch (3 mm) thick and cut into triangles. • Spread the cheese, olives, and onion mixture on each triangle. Season with pepper and drizzle with the remaining oil. • Transfer the triangles to the baking sheet. • Bake until the pizza dough is golden brown, about 15 minutes. • Serve hot or at room temperature.

1 quantity pizza dough (see page 32)
4 medium red onions
3/4 cup (180 ml) water
4 tablespoons extra-virgin olive oil
1 tablespoon finely chopped thyme
1 tablespoon finely chopped rosemary
Salt and freshly ground black pepper
1 1/4 cups (310 g) fresh creamy cheese
   (goat cheese, mozzarella, stracchino)
4–6 tablespoons pitted black olives

Cheese Savories
with onion and olives

Prepare the pizza dough. • Preheat the oven to 450°F (225°C/gas 8). • Oil 2 large baking sheets. • Heat the oil and butter in a medium frying pan over medium heat. Sauté the onion until softened, about 5 minutes. • Roll out the dough on a lightly floured work surface into a large square about ½ inch (1 cm) thick. • Sprinkle the dough with the onion mixture, cheese, olives, and anchovies, if using. • Roll the dough up carefully into a log. • Cut into ½-inch (1-cm) thick slices. Place on the prepared baking sheets, making sure they are well spaced. • Bake until risen and golden brown, about 20 minutes. • Serve hot or at room temperature.

1 quantity pizza dough (see page 32)
2 tablespoons extra-virgin olive oil
1 tablespoon butter
1 large white onion, finely chopped
1 cup (120 g) freshly grated emmenthal or Cheddar cheese
2 oz (60 g) black olives, pitted and chopped
4 anchovy fillets, chopped (optional)

SERVES 6

PREPARATION 15 min

COOKING 15 min

DIFFICULTY level 1

Chicken Satay

Place the shallots, garlic, chilies, ginger, coriander, peppercorns, candlenuts, shrimp paste, and cloves in a food processor and chop until smooth. • Heat the oil in a wok or saucepan over medium-high heat and sauté the spicy mixture for 5 minutes. Set aside to cool. • Place the chicken in a bowl with the spicy mixture, coconut, lime juice, salt, pepper, and chilies and mix well. • Press the chicken mixture around 12 wooden skewers and grill over a barbecue or under a preheated broiler (grill) until the chicken is well cooked, 10–15 minutes. • Serve hot.

6 shallots
6 cloves garlic
1–2 fresh red chile peppers, sliced
1-inch (2.5-cm) piece ginger root, peeled
2 teaspoons coriander seeds
1 teaspoon black peppercorns
3 candlenuts
1 teaspoon dried shrimp paste
2 cloves
3 tablespoons peanut oil
1½ lb (750 g) ground (minced) chicken breast
1 cup (150 g) freshly grated coconut
2 tablespoons fresh lime juice
Salt and freshly ground black pepper
2 dried chile peppers, crumbled

SERVES 6–8

PREPARATION 15 min

COOKING 20 min

DIFFICULTY level 1

Beef Skewers
with spicy sauce

Place the beef in a large bowl and stir in the mint and parsley. Season with salt and pepper. • Shape into balls about the size of a walnut and flatten slightly. • Preheat the broiler (grill) on high setting. • Heat the oil in a medium frying pan over medium heat. Sauté the onion and bell pepper until softened, about 5 minutes. • Add the water, ketchup, Tabasco, sugar, and vinegar. Season with salt and pepper. • Thread the beef balls onto wooden skewers—2 or 3 per skewer—and cook under the broiler (or over the glowing embers of a barbecue) until golden brown and cooked through, about 10 minutes. • Serve hot with the spicy sauce.

1½ lb (750 g) ground (minced) beef
Salt and freshly ground black pepper
1 tablespoon finely chopped mint
1 tablespoon finely chopped parsley
¼ cup (60 ml) extra-virgin olive oil
½ small bell yellow pepper (capsicum)
1 medium white onion, finely chopped
¼ cup (60 ml) water
½ cup (125 ml) ketchup
1 teaspoon Tabasco sauce
½ teaspoon sugar
1 teaspoon vinegar

Beef Skewers
with snow peas

Place the beef in a large bowl and stir in the onion, garlic, chile pepper, and parsley. Season with salt and pepper. • Shape into balls about the size of a walnut. • Preheat the broiler (grill) on high setting. • Heat the water and oil in a large frying pan over medium heat. carefully add the meatballs and simmer until cooked through, 8–10 minutes. • Cook the snow peas in a small pan of salted water until just tender, about 5 minutes. Drain well. • Thread the beef balls onto wooden skewers—3 or 4 per skewer—alternating each meatball with a piece of snow pea. • Season the yogurt with salt, pepper, and mint. • Serve the skewers hot with the yogurt sauce.

1½ lb (750 g) ground (minced) beef
1 small white onion, finely chopped
1 clove garlic, finely chopped
1 dry red chile pepper, crumbled
1 tablespoon finely chopped parsley
Salt and freshly ground black pepper
8–10 snow peas (sugar peas),
    cut into short lengths
½ cup (125 ml) water
¼ cup (60 ml) extra-virgin olive oil
1½ cups (375 g) plain yogurt
1 tablespoon finely chopped mint

SERVES 6–8

PREPARATION 10 min

COOKING 15 min

DIFFICULTY level 1

Beef Dumplings
with ginger and soy sauce

Blanch the cabbage leaf in sated boiling water for 2 minutes. Drain and remove the tough central stem. Chop finely. • Place the beef in a large bowl. Add the scallions, parsley, egg whites, cornstarch, ginger, sugar, sherry, soy sauce, cabbage, and paprika. Mix well. • Shape the mixture into balls the size of large walnuts. • Moisten a large piece of waxed paper, prick holes in it using the tines of a fork and brush lightly with oil. • Line a steamer with the prepared paper and then add the meatballs. Steam, turning from time to time, until cooked through, about 15 minutes. • Serve hot.

1 large Savoy cabbage leaf

1½ lb (750 g) ground (minced) beef

2 scallions (green onions), finely chopped

1 tablespoon finely chopped parsley

2 large egg whites

1 tablespoon cornstarch (cornflour)

1 tablespoon freshly grated root ginger

1 teaspoon sugar

1 tablespoon dry sherry or sake

⅓ cup (90 ml) dark soy sauce

½ teaspoon hot paprika

SERVES 8–10

PREPARATION 15 min

COOKING 20 min

DIFFICULTY level 1

Potato Fritters
with ricotta and oats

Preheat the oven to 350°F (180°C/gas 4). • Place the potato in a large bowl. Add the oats, ricotta, egg, Parmesan, parsley, and sesame seeds. Season with salt and pepper. Add enough of the milk to make a soft dough. • Shape the mixture into balls the size of walnuts. • Dip the balls in the egg yolks, followed by the bread crumbs, then flatten slightly. • Arrange on an oiled baking sheet and drizzle with the oil. • Bake until lightly browned, about 20 minutes. • Serve hot.

2 cups (400 g) mashed potato
$3\frac{1}{2}$ cups (350 g) old-fashioned rolled oats
$\frac{3}{4}$ cup (180 g) ricotta cheese, drained
1 large egg, lightly beaten
2 tablespoons freshly grated Parmesan
2 tablespoons finely chopped parsley
2 tablespoon sesame seeds
Salt and freshly ground white pepper
$\frac{1}{3}$ cup (90 ml) milk
2 large egg yolks, lightly beaten
1 cup (150 g) fine dry bread crumbs
$\frac{1}{4}$ cup (60 ml) extra-virgin olive oil

Meatballs
with sesame seeds

Soak the bread in the milk in a large bowl. • Drain well, squeezing out the excess milk. Break the bread into pieces. • Add the beef, egg, parsley, garlic, and nutmeg and mix well. Season with salt and pepper. • Shape the mixture into balls the size of walnuts. • Press a piece of Mozzarella and bell pepper into the center of each meatball. Close up the meatball. • Place the sesame seeds on a plate. Roll the meatballs in the sesame seeds, coating well. • Heat the oil in a deep-fryer or frying pan to very hot. • Fry the fritters in batches until golden brown all over. Remove with a slotted spoon and drain on paper towels. • Serve hot.

3 slices sandwich bread, crusts removed

1/3 cup (90 ml) milk

1 1/2 lb (750 g) ground (minced) beef

1 large egg, lightly beaten

2 tablespoons finely chopped parsley

1/2 clove garlic, finely chopped

1/4 teaspoon freshly grated nutmeg

Salt and freshly ground black pepper

4 oz (125 g) Mozzarella cheese, cut into small cubes

2 large pieces red bell pepper (capsicum) preserved in oil, drained and cut into small cubes

4 tablespoons sesame seeds

2 cups (500 ml) olive oil, for frying

Apricot Fritters
with pork and marsala

Put the apricots in a bowl and add the Marsala. Leave to soak for 2 hours. • Preheat the oven to 425°F (220°C/gas 7). • Place the meat in a large bowl. Add the parsley, garlic, nutmeg, and paprika. Season with salt and pepper, and mix well. • Drain the apricots and make an incision in each one. Fill the apricots with the meat mixture. Close each one over the filling. • Beat the egg whites and cornstarch with a pinch of salt in a bowl to make a smooth batter. • Heat the oil in a large frying pan over medium heat. Dip the stuffed apricots in the egg mixture and then drop into the hot oil. Fry until golden brown all over, about 10 minutes. • Drain on paper towels. • Arrange on an oiled baking sheet and bake for 10 minutes, until the meat is cooked through. • Serve hot.

12 dried apricots
$\frac{1}{3}$ cup (90 ml) dry Marsala
8 oz (250 g) lean ground (minced) pork
2 tablespoons finely chopped parsley
1 clove garlic, finely chopped
$\frac{1}{2}$ teaspoon freshly grated nutmeg
$\frac{1}{2}$ teaspoon hot paprika or 1 dry chile pepper, crumbled
Salt and freshly ground black pepper
2 large egg whites
2 tablespoons cornstarch (cornflour)
1 cup (250 ml) olive oil, for frying

SERVES 6–8

PREPARATION 10 min

COOKING 20 min

DIFFICULTY level 1

Spinach Frittata
with cherry tomatoes

Preheat the oven to 400°F (200°C/gas 6). • Oil a 10 inch (25 cm) square baking dish. • Cook the spinach in a medium saucepan of lightly salted water over medium heat until tender, 3–5 minutes. Drain well and squeeze out the excess moisture. Chop coarsely. • Break 5 of the eggs into a large bowl and beat until frothy. Add the Parmesan and season with salt and pepper. Mix well then pour the mixture into the prepared dish. • Bake until the egg is set, 5–10 minutes. • Break the remaining eggs into a large bowl and beat until frothy. Add the spinach and season with salt and pepper. Mix well. • Remove the frittata from the oven and spread with the spinach mixture. Place the tomatoes on top and bake for 5 minutes more, or until cooked through. • Cut into squares and serve hot.

2 lb (1 kg) frozen spinach
7 large eggs
$\frac{1}{2}$ cup (60 g) freshly grated Parmesan
Salt and freshly ground black pepper
6 cherry tomatoes, thinly sliced

SERVES 6–8

PREPARATION 15 min

COOKING 20 min

DIFFICULTY level 1

Ricotta Fritters

Mix together the Ricotta, fresh bread crumbs, Parmesan, parsley, and salt in a large bowl. • Shape the mixture into balls the size of walnuts. Roll the balls in the dry bread crumbs. • Heat the oil in a deep-fryer or frying pan to very hot. • Fry the fritters in batches until golden brown all over. Remove with a slotted spoon and drain on paper towels. • Serve hot.

1½ cups (375 g) ricotta cheese, drained
2½ cups (200 g) fresh bread crumbs
½ cup (60 g) freshly grated Parmesan
1 tablespoon finely chopped parsley
Salt
½ cup (60 g) fine dry bread crumbs
2 cups (500 ml) frying oil

Cheese Fritters

Place three egg whites in a medium bowl with a pinch of salt and beat until stiff peaks form. • Fold in both cheeses. Add half the flour. Season with salt and pepper. • Shape the mixture into balls the size of walnuts. • Beat the remaining egg and yolk. • Dip the fritters in the egg. Roll in the remaining flour and then in the bread crumbs. Heat the oil in a deep-fryer or frying pan to very hot. • Fry the fritters in batches until golden brown all over. Remove with a slotted spoon and drain on paper towels. • Serve hot.

2 large eggs + 2 large egg whites
Salt and freshly ground white pepper
8 oz (250 g) freshly grated Gruyère or Cheddar cheese
6 tablespoons freshly grated Parmesan
$\frac{1}{2}$ cup (100 g) all-purpose (plain) flour
2 cups (500 ml) frying oil
1 cup (150 g) fine dry bread crumbs

Baked Cheese
balls

Place all the ingredients in a large bowl and mix well, adding enough extra milk to make a smooth, firm dough. • Shape the dough into a ball. • Wrap in plastic wrap (cling film) and chill in the refrigerator for 30 minutes. • Preheat the oven to 400°F (200°C/gas 6). • Oil three baking sheets. • Shape the dough into balls about the size of a walnut. Arrange on the prepared baking sheets. • Bake until golden brown, about 15 minutes. • Serve warm.

1 cup (250 g) ricotta cheese, drained

$\frac{2}{3}$ cup (100 g) whole-wheat (wholemeal) flour

2 tablespoons bran, toasted

2 cups (300 g) all-purpose (plain) flour

$\frac{1}{4}$ cup (60 ml) extra-virgin olive oil

$\frac{3}{4}$ cup (90 g) freshly grated Parmesan

1$\frac{1}{2}$ teaspoons baking powder

$\frac{1}{2}$ teaspoon salt

$\frac{1}{4}$ cup (60 ml) milk + extra, as required

SERVES 6–8

PREPARATION 45 min + 2 h for dough

COOKING 30 min

DIFFICULTY level 3

Fritters

with mozzarella and tomatoes

Prepare the pizza dough. • Blanch the tomatoes in boiling water for 2 minutes. Drain and peel. Chop the tomatoes, discarding the seeds. • Place the anchovies, tomatoes, mozzarella, and oregano in a bowl. Season with salt and pepper, mix well. • Roll out the dough on a lightly floured work surface to ¼ inch (5 mm) thick. Cut it into 4-inch (10-cm) disks using a large glass or cookie cutter. • Place a little of the filling in the center of each disk. Moisten the edges of the dough and fold it in half to cover the filling. Pinch the edges together to seal. Heat the oil in a deep-fryer or frying pan to very hot. • Fry the fritters in batches until puffed and golden brown. Remove with a slotted spoon and drain on paper towels. • Serve hot.

1 quantity pizza dough (see page 32)
14 oz (400 g) firm ripe tomatoes
4 anchovy fillets, chopped
6 oz (180 g) fresh mozzarella cheese, cut into small cubes
1 teaspoon dried oregano
Salt and freshly ground black pepper
2 cups (500 ml) oil, for frying

Savory Puffs

Set the pastry cases out on a serving platter. • Cheese filling: Beat the mascarpone and Gorgonzola in a medium bowl. Add the milk if the mixture is too thick. Season with salt and pepper. • Onion and egg filling: Cook the onion in the vegetable stock in a small saucepan over medium heat for 5 minutes. Transfer to a food processor with the goat cheese and eggs and process until smooth. Season with salt and pepper. • Ham and ricotta filling: Mix the chopped ham into the Ricotta. Season with salt and pepper. • Make any—or all—of these fillings. Place them in a pastry bag with a plain tip and fill the pastry cases. • Serve as soon as possible after filling otherwise the pastry will turn soggy.

20–25 storebought choux pastry cases (as used for cream puffs)

Cheese Filling
1/2 cup (125 g) mascarpone or cream cheese
4 oz (125 g) Gorgonzola or other soft blue cheese, crumbled
1–2 tablespoons milk, as required
Salt and freshly ground black pepper

Onion and Egg Filling
1 large onion, finely chopped
4 tablespoons vegetable stock (homemade or bouillon cube)
3/4 cup (180 g) soft goat cheese
2 soft-boiled eggs

Ham and Cheese Filling
3/4 cup (90 g) finely chopped ham
1/2 cup (125 g) ricotta cheese, drained

Parmesan Fritters

Place the flour, salt, and baking powder in a large bowl and mix well. • Add half the butter and use your fingertips to work it into the flour. • Pour in enough water to obtain a firm dough. • Place the dough out on a lightly floured work surface and knead for 5 minutes. • Use a rolling pin to flatten the dough into a sheet about ⅛ inch (3 mm) thick. • Place pieces of Parmesan on one half of the dough about 2 inches (5 cm) apart. Top each piece of cheese with a piece of the remaining butter. • Fold the piece of dough without cheese on it over the other half. • Use a pastry cutter or sharp knife to cut out rectangles around each piece of cheese. Heat the oil in a deep-fryer or frying pan to very hot. • Fry the fritters in batches until golden brown all over. Remove with a slotted spoon and drain on paper towels. • Serve hot.

3 cups (450 g) all-purpose (plain) flour
Salt
5 oz (150 g) Parmesan cheese, thinly sliced
5 oz (150 g) butter. chopped
½ cup (125 ml) warm water
1 teaspoon baking powder
2 cups (500 ml) oil, for frying

SERVES 6–8

PREPARATION 15 min

COOKING 50 min

DIFFICULTY level 2

Cod Fritters
with poppy seeds

Boil the potatoes in a pot of salted boiling water until tender, 20–25 minutes. Drain and mash until smooth. • Heat the oil in a frying pan over medium heat. Sauté the cod and garlic until the cod is cooked, about 5 minutes. • Mash the fish and garlic with a fork and add to the potatoes. Stir in the poppy seeds, egg, bread, chives, salt and pepper, and mix well. • Shape the mixture into fritters about the size of a walnut. • Heat the oil in a deep-fryer or frying pan to very hot. • Fry the fritters in batches until golden brown all over. Remove with a slotted spoon and drain on paper towels. • Serve hot.

1 lb (500 g) potatoes, peeled
2 tablespoons extra-virgin olive oil
12 oz (350 g) cod fillets, chopped
1 clove garlic, finely chopped
3 tablespoons poppy seeds
1 large egg. lightly beaten
6 slices sandwich bread, crusts removed and crumbled
2 tablespoons finely chopped chives
Salt and freshly ground white pepper
2 cups (500 ml) frying oil

SERVES 6–8

PREPARATION 15 min

COOKING 30 min

DIFFICULTY level 2

Pea Fritters
with cheese

Boil the peas in a large pot of salted boiling water until tender, about 10 minutes. • Chop in a food processor until smooth. • Place in a bowl and stir in the rice flour, ricotta, Parmesan, basil, and marjoram. Season with salt and pepper and mix well. • Shape the mixture into fritters about the size of a walnut. Dredge in the flour, dip in the beaten egg, and roll in the bread crumbs. • Heat the oil in a deep-fryer or frying pan to very hot. • Fry the fritters in batches until golden brown all over. Remove with a slotted spoon and drain on paper towels. • Serve hot.

1 lb (500 g) frozen peas
1 cup (150 g) rice flour
$\frac{1}{2}$ cup (125 g) ricotta cheese, drained
$\frac{1}{2}$ cup (60 g) freshly grated Parmesan
1 tablespoon finely chopped basil
1 tablespoon finely chopped marjoram
Salt and freshly ground black pepper
$\frac{1}{3}$ cup (50 g) all-purpose (plain) flour
1 large egg, lightly beaten
$\frac{1}{2}$ cup (75 g) fine dry bread crumbs
2 cups (500 ml) frying oil

Index

Copyright © 2007 by McRae Books Srl

This English edition first published in 2007

All rights reserved. No part of this book may be reproduced in any form without the prior written permission of the publisher and copyright owner.

Finger Food

was created and produced by McRae Books Srl

Borgo Santa Croce, 8 – Florence (Italy)

info@mcraebooks.com

Publishers: Anne McRae and Marco Nardi

Project Director: Anne McRae

Design: Sara Mathews

Text: Carla Bardi

Editing: Osla Fraser

Photography: Mauro Corsi, Leonardo Pasquinelli, Gianni Petronio, Lorenzo Borri, Stefano Pratesi

Home Economist: Benedetto Rillo

Artbuying: McRae Books

Layouts: Adina Stefania Dragomir

Repro: Fotolito Raf, Florence

ISBN 978-88-89272-93-0

Printed and bound in China